Field Manual for Discouraged Democrats

Survival Guide and Recovery Handbook

S.R. Kennedy, Ed.

Hedgehog House Books

Field Manual for Discouraged Democrats © 2026 by S. Ridgway Kennedy Doe is licensed under CC BY-SA 4.0.

Creative Commons Attribution-ShareAlike 4.0 International

This license requires that reusers give credit to the creator. It allows reusers to distribute, remix, adapt, and build upon the material in any medium or format, even for commercial purposes. If others remix, adapt, or build upon the material, they must license the modified material under identical terms.

BY: Credit must be given to S. R. Kennedy and Hedgehog House Books.

SA: Adaptations must be shared under the same terms.

To view a copy of this license, visit https://creativecommons.org/licenses/by-sa/4.0/

"Naturally, the common people don't want war... but it is always a simple matter to drag the people along. All you have to do is tell them they are being attacked."
— *Hermann Göring*

"War does not determine who is right—only who is left."
— *Bertrand Russell*

"All war is a symptom of man's failure as a thinking animal."
— *John Steinbeck*

"Politics and war are remarkably similar situations."
— *Newt Gingrich*

"When all else fails, read the instructions."
— Anonymous

FM 2025-1116A

Restricted Distribution: This document, prepared under the auspices of advocates for democracy and is restricted for reading only by individuals who ascribe to fundamental democratic practices and principles established by our founding documents and evolved over time to include democratic representation in government as well as respect and adherence to the rule of law. Persons opposed to fundamental decency and democracy in the United States of America are not, under any circumstances, permitted to access this material on penalty of engaging in unacceptable collusion with radical left enemies of the people.

Department for Defense of Democracy
Morale and Encouragement Division

TABLE OF CONTENTS

General Washington's Situation Report (SITREP)

Glossary

1. Fear Less

2. Take Care of Yourself

3. Reestablish the Chain of Command

4. Conduct a Thorough After-Action Report (AAR)

5. Know Your Enemy

6. Know and Support Your Allies

7. Intelligence, Intelligence, Intelligence

8. Rules of Engagement

9. Strategy & Tactics

10. Marching Orders

Subject: Defending Our Experiment in Democracy
From: G. Washington, General, Ret., Continental Army
To: All Personnel—The Troops Defending the Arsenal of Democracy, The United States of America

Soldiers, your dedication and sacrifice are recognized. We have reached a critical phase in our operation. Our mission, conducted in 2024, was organized to lead our nation further toward our ideals related to life, liberty, and the pursuit of happiness. It ended in a significant defeat. You can be assured that everyone on the general staff of the Democratic Resistance Force is working diligently to gather battlefield intelligence (voting data) and any other helpful information. They are analyzing our tactical and strategic failures. As a part of the After Action Review, they are also assessing how our opponent outmaneuvered or outperformed friendly forces.

And so, let me assure you—our best civilian minds have joined with our best generals to prepare for the next battle. And you can be certain, as a defender of Democracy, that there will be more battles.

Situation Overview

From my position, I have an excellent view of the terrain and a clear perspective on how our operations are being supported on the home front. There is no doubt in my mind that our great American experiment in democracy is facing a severe test.

There can no longer be any doubt. Americans are at war with themselves, and the future of democracy is at stake.

Throughout our history, when we faced great challenges, Americans pulled themselves together. Yes, we had our struggles along the way. The Civil War? What a terrible time. I thought that President Lincoln handled that as well as possible. As a Virginian and a slave owner on the one hand, and in my role as a "Founding Father," I was appalled by the conflict and carnage. I thank God that I didn't have to choose a side.

I was appalled by the atrocities of WWI. Machine guns? Gas attacks? General Pershing and his men. Some people called it "the war to end all wars." If only they had been right.

America's performance in World War II placed us in a remarkable position. We were, truly, the arsenal of democracy. Our former adversaries, Germany and Japan became more than "allies." They are our partners. Our friends.

The Rising Threat

It is difficult for me to imagine what you are going through today. In my time, when we planned, discussed, and debated matters, we spoke to each other. We treated one another as colleagues. In general, we were friends, or at least friendly. Of course, there were hotheads. Burr. Jackson. Dueling? The stupidity of it. And yet, looking at our current ranks, I see and hear officers in our ranks shouting down and insulting each other in public. What is that? It is a weakness that our adversaries will exploit.

I am, I admit, perplexed by the swirling cauldron you refer to as the Internet. It is unfathomable that one person can, in a moment or two, attempt direct communication with a million or more other people. The magnitude of the messages, moving instantly from place to place, is beyond my comprehension.

I am aware, however, of assaults on people carried out by use of the Internet: anonymous threats and malicious behavior. It is, simply, bullying and something no responsible person would condone. Yet, it goes on. It reminds me of stories about German mobs in the days leading up to World War II. Large groups of thuggish men—I think they were called Brownshirts—acting violently against their own citizens.

The Democratic Dilemma

As you consider your actions going forward, it is critical that you understand the greatest strength and the greatest weakness of democracy. Voting gives people the power to choose their own destiny. With that power, they can choose to end democracy.

Hugo Chávez was elected in 1998. Look at Venezuela today. Recep Tayyip Erdoğan won a democratic election as Prime Minister in 2003. Later he became President. For life? Viktor Orbán, elected in 2010, has turned Hungary into an authoritarian state. And since his first election in 2000, Vladimir Putin has transformed Russia from a shambling democracy back into a Tsardom where one man rules all.

From my distant perspective, that looks like four very good examples of nations where people willingly voted to do away with their own democratic rights.

The Constitution

When we wrote The Constitution, I thought we did a pretty good job. But it was difficult because so much compromise was required. We had to build it to accommodate slavery. That was the reality of our day. All the mechanics of elections and especially the presidential election, were designed to bring Southern enslavers, men like me, I confess, into agreement with Northern bankers. The results were messy. The Electoral College, for example, was a crazy idea that Jim Wilson from Pennsylvania cooked up. Electors, he believed, would protect our government from *too much* democratic influence.

I can see today how the concessions we made in the document to accommodate the enslavement of people have become a terrible, potentially fatal liability in our effort to create a stable government.

You know what our ideals are. We stated them clearly in The Declaration and The Constitution. And yes, they were aspirational. We weren't perfect. The work was flawed. But we did succeed in guiding the ship of state in the right direction. That's a poor analogy for an old Army man, but everything about what we did back then was happening fast. We made it up as we went along. And deep in our hearts, we believed in the ideals of liberty, justice, equality and democracy. We added safety measures specifically to prevent authoritarian rule. You can see that in the "checks and balances," as political scientists call them, we devised in the Constitution and the Bill of Rights.

The government we set up was jury-rigged. It was overly complicated and confusing. However, and I beg of you to give us credit for this, it worked reasonably well for well more than two centuries.

Until now.

When I was asked to prepare this SITREP—military jargon for a Situation Report—I was honored. It has become increasingly difficult to remain an impartial observer.

Some of you may remember what I said in my *"Farewell Address."* That was what the press labeled it. The title Hamilton gave it was "The Address of Gen. Washington to the People on His Declining the Presidency of the United

States." Yes, Alexander was the one who wrote down the words, but they reflect what I believed. He knew my mind.

On Political Parties:

This is what I said in my *Farewell Address*:

The common and continual mischiefs of the spirit of party are sufficient to make it the interest and duty of a wise people to discourage and restrain it.

Imagine that. Encouraging restraint on political parties. Thinking there ought to be some limits on what they can do, say, or spend?

On National Unity:

From the *Farewell address:*

The unity of government which constitutes you one people is also now dear to you. It is justly so; for it is a main pillar in the edifice of your real independence.

In retrospect, that seems a little wordy. The motto we came up with in '76, *E pluribus unum*, says it better: "Out of many, one." What we had in mind was the idea that we were a diverse group of people, we Americans. In order to be strong, we needed to be able to understand each other, look past our differences, and unite in striving for the good of us all.

On Foreign Influence:

And this:

Observe good faith and justice towards all nations; cultivate peace and harmony with all.

During my presidency, we had to navigate the aftermath of our revolution. For a tiny nation, it was a perilous journey. Our relationship with England was hardly cordial. Our close relationship with France was upended by their revolution. We had to maintain a good relationship with Spain to secure navigation rights on the Mississippi River and access to New Orleans.

Maintaining good diplomatic relations is a complicated business. There is, however, one thing I can assure you about. When you have an ally like France was during our revolution, you respect, honor, and support them. Our independence would not have been achieved in 1781 if we had not had France at our side.

So, as I say farewell again, I'll advise you to do everything you can to strengthen your relationships with your true, democratic allies. You know who they are. *E pluribus unum* is a fitting motto for international relations, I believe. It certainly mattered when your military was fighting World War II.

Final Thoughts

This *Field Manual* has been prepared to help you reassemble and reform your ranks after the disaster of the 2024 Campaign. It contains survival strategies, ideas about how to reassemble your units, and it addresses our mission and purpose.

The *Manual* is designed to help you prepare for the next battle. It encourages you to assess your enemy. You need a clear understanding of who or what your real enemy is. Intelligence gathering is required. This little book will deal with strategy, tactics, the weapons at your disposal, and the rules of engagement.

Most importantly, the *Manual* will offer encouragement.

Yes, you can make a difference in this unfortunate New Civil War. The Red Team versus the Blue Team? It sounds like some children's playground exercise. And yet, it is a contest that may have a profound impact on the future of our great nation.

I can remember the dark days at Valley Forge, when we Continentals, as we called ourselves, were hunkered down, simply trying to survive the winter. You may be feeling a little like we did on those dark days.

Be sure, soldiers. Spring is coming. Significant electoral conflicts will soon be at hand. They may be nearly a year away, but they are coming. The defenders of our experiment in democracy will reassemble. We will go into battle again. Stronger. Smarter. Tougher.

We *will* stand by our principles. We *will* support our Democratic ideals. We *will* eschew anger and embrace reason. We *will* uphold the inalienable rights of all human beings. We *will* champion justice. We *will* defend our planet against the unintentional but profound impact of human activity. We *will* oppose, with all our strength, the corrosive influence of selfish ambition, corruption, and greed.

Go forward with clear eyes and full hearts. You are standing on the side of democracy.

E pluribus unum.

G. Washington

GLOSSARY

Angertainment – A billion-dollar industry designed to profit from outrage, anger, and misinformation. Angertainment media and angertainers (frequently referenced as "political influencers") make their living based on clicks, retweets, and similar online activity. In their business, the number one source for "engagement" is anger. They promote rage at enemies and use real-time data from online activity to test their divisive messages, aim, and fire them at likely targets while their devoted audience applauds. Angertainment is a corrosive force eating away at the heart of American democracy.

ASAP – Acronym for All States Are Purple. Journalists and angertainers alike use the terms "Red State" and "Blue State" to refer to the political leanings of individual states. When the electoral control of the state could go one way or the other, they refer to these states as "purple." The red state/blue state referencing effectively ignores very large numbers of voters. Even in the reddest of red states, some votes are cast for the minority party in that state. In reality, every state is purple.

Decimation – A word that is frequently misused in contrast to its original meaning. Modern writers use it as a synonym for devastation, annihilation, obliteration, and words like that. In fact, the word originated in ancient Rome and refers to a brutal disciplinary practice in the Roman Legions. In rare circumstances, a unit that was accused of cowardice, mutiny, or desertion, might be "decimated." Decimation required one out of every ten soldiers to be put to death by the other soldiers in the unit.

Democracy – A system of government which, in its pure form, power rest in the hands of the people who are eligible to vote. Power rests directly with the people and citizens vote on directly on laws and policies. Historic example: ancient Athens.

Democrat – A member or supporter of the Democratic Party, one of the two major political parties in the United States. Historically associated with support for social programs, civil rights, environmental protection, and a more active role for government in addressing social and economic issues.

Democratic Republic – A hybrid system of government where citizens elect representatives as in a republic, but the government is accountable to democratic principles. A democratic republic balances majority rule with constitutional protections. However, if the system of checks and balances weakens, a democratic republic can slide toward either majority tyranny or authoritarianism. The United

States today is considered a democratic republic—citizens elect leaders. Historically, the Constitution has limited government power and protected citizen's rights.

Engagement – In the digital media world, a metric measuring clicks, views, shares, comments, and time spent on content. Social media platforms and angertainment outlets use engagement as their primary measure of success, regardless of the accuracy or impact of the content. Higher engagement means more advertising revenue. Anger generates the highest engagement.

False Equivalency – A logical fallacy that occurs when two opposing arguments appear to be logically equivalent when in fact they are not. In political discourse, this often manifests when media outlets give equal weight to a substantiated claim and an unsubstantiated one in the name of "balance."

Four-Way Test – Rotary International's ethical guide for personal and professional conduct; a simple, universal framework for integrity, fairness, and positive impact used by 1.4 million people in more than 200 countries. Before speaking or acting, answer the following. Is it the truth? Is it fair to all concerned? Will it build goodwill and better friendships? Will it be beneficial to all concerned?

Gerrymander – The practice of manipulating the boundaries of electoral districts to favor one party or class. Named after Elbridge Gerry, whose party drew a salamander-shaped district in Massachusetts in 1812. Modern gerrymandering uses sophisticated data analysis to create districts that dilute opposition voting power.

Golden Rule – Refers to the ethical guideline present in most religions and philosophies that people should treat other people the way they themselves want to be treated.

Greed – Excessive desire for wealth or power, often at the expense of others. In the context of this manual, greed represents one of the primary motivating forces behind threats to democracy, driving both individual and institutional behavior that undermines democratic principles and the common good.

Grover Grovel – Reference to the *Taxpayer Protection Pledge* created by Grover Norquist's Americans for Tax Reform, which commits signatories to oppose any and all tax increases. Many Republican politicians have signed this pledge, effectively limiting their ability to compromise on fiscal policy regardless of circumstances.

Hypocritic Oath – References the requirement for elected representatives to say and/or do things and then criticize others for doing the same thing. It highlights the frequently visible disconnect between stated Republican principles and actual practices, particularly regarding fiscal responsibility, family values, and constitutional governance.

Hubris – Excessive pride or self-confidence, often leading to downfall or punishment. The word hubris comes from ancient Greek, where it referred to a dangerous overstepping of bounds—especially when mortals defied the gods. In modern usage, it describes a kind of arrogant overconfidence that blinds someone to risks, consequences, or ethical limits. Persons with hubris have exaggerated pride, self-confidence and believe in their own superiority that goes beyond reason. This is accompanied by arrogance and pretension and often combined with a dismissive attitude toward others, social conventions, or rules.

Journalism – The activity or profession of gathering, assessing, creating, and presenting news and information. Real journalism involves verification of facts, consideration of multiple sources, editorial oversight, and accountability. It stands in contrast to propaganda, entertainment, and angertainment, which may present themselves as journalism but lack these essential elements.

Manipulation – The act of controlling or influencing someone or something in a clever or unethical way. In political contexts, manipulation involves the use of propaganda, disinformation, emotional appeals, and psychological tactics to influence public opinion and behavior without regard for truth or the public good.

Maslow's Hammer – Also known as the law of the instrument. A cognitive bias where people rely too heavily on familiar tools or approaches, even when they might not be the best fit for a problem. "If all you have is a hammer, everything looks like a nail." In political discourse, this describes the tendency to apply the same solutions or arguments to every problem.

RAFF – Acronym for "Reject Anger, Fight Fear." The foundational principle of this field manual, emphasizing the importance of maintaining emotional discipline and strategic clarity in the face of adversity.

Republic – A republic is government by elected representatives, constrained by laws or a constitution to protect rights. Historic example: ancient Rome.

Republican – A member or supporter of the Republican Party, one of the two major political parties in the United States. Historically associated with free-market capitalism, limited government, strong national defense, and traditional social values. The party has undergone significant transformation in recent years.

SITREP – Military abbreviation for "Situation Report." A concise summary of the current tactical and strategic situation, typically including friendly and enemy positions, terrain assessment, and operational status.

Social Capital; Social Capitalism – A concept popularized by Robert Putmnam in his book *Bowling Alone*. Putnam makes the case for the importance of simple human interactions like being members of a bowling league team, a drama society or a bridge club. Social capital reinforces trust between individuals. It is a powerful force, but it is on the wane as more people spend more and more time online or otherwise being too busy to have strong relationships with other people in real life. Pierre Bourdieu and James Coleman are two other names to look for in researching social capital.

WAIT – Acronym for "Why Am I Talking?" A tactical reminder to listen more than you speak, particularly when engaging in any discussion including conversations about political views and objectives. Active listening often reveals more useful intelligence than passionate argument.

WAIST – Acronym for "Why Am I Sharing This?" A tactical reminder to pause before taking action, especially when online and sharing, liking, commenting and otherwise "sharing." Before sharing apply the Rotary International four-way test or some other ethical filter. Significant amounts of online content are purposely engineered to provoke fear and anger for profit. Determine where you stand in relation to the possibility of spreading fear and anger while increasing their profits before clicking. WAIST prevents waste.

Weird/Weirding – Weird, as an adjective, references something odd, unusual, different, or outside of an observer's experience. In primitive societies, weirdness may be taboo. Individuals may be ostracized for being weird. In contemporary American culture, weirdness can result in gross misunderstandings. One person may may take offense at some kind of weirdness. Another person may laugh and simply note that it is weird. Weirding, turning weird into a verb, describes the reaction some people may have to perceived weirdness. A great deal of conflict and anger results from people who are exposed to weirdness and take offense at it, simply because it is not part of their experience. Angertainment capitalizes on weirdness to turn it into a cause for fear, disgust, anger, and outrage.

Chapter 1
FEAR LESS

Anyone who says they *do not* fear for the future of American Democracy is not paying attention to what is actually happening. Any sensible friend of American democracy is afraid. We do not know what is going to happen, but based on the first year of the second Trump administration, we know it is going to challenge our democratic norms.

We are afraid and we should be. The current administration wants us to be afraid. The people in charge of it are succeeding beyond their high expectations.

Understand this: Fear is an essential ingredient and precursor to anger. Fear and anger go together. Fear creates flammable situations. Then, perhaps through spontaneous combustion or because someone ignites a fuse, fear can burst into anger.

Your success in the coming campaign season requires you to acknowledge your fear and learn to set it aside. This will not be easy. You must do this, however, because fear and the anger it provokes are the primary weapons your adversaries are employing in their war on democracy.

Your adversaries have successfully used fear and anger as a powerful wedge that is dividing Americans against themselves. They have found ways to benefit financially from their campaign tactics. And while they foment partisanship and anger, they are enabling the hubris and greed to flourish.

There is nothing new in the idea behind this kind of warfare. Angry threats and intimidation for been used as weapons by bullies forever. What is new to this war, however, is the technology driving their campaign of fear, anger, and mistrust.

This *Manual* will describe some of the ways that fear is created, amplified, and disseminated. For now, understand that every one of us is afraid. Under the circumstances, we cannot be fearless. Instead, we must fear less. We must set our very real fears aside and look our enemy straight in the eye.

Anger Is Your Greatest Enemy

"Those whom the gods would destroy, first they make mad."

Attributions for this phrase are associated with classical literature and philosophy dating back more than 2000 years. Though variations are found in ancient Greek texts, the exact origin is unclear. The idea reflects the theme of hubris—excessive pride or arrogance—that can blind someone and lead to their downfall. In this operation, it also addresses the idea of anger directly.

If a soldier wants to serve effectively, it is vitally important to keep emotions in check. Stay calm. Assess the situation. Keep anger under control.

This is a war, not just a battle. It will not end with a truce or peace agreement. It will end when the opposing party returns to sanity and supports democracy, or when democracy is finally crushed in the United States of America. Your mission is to decide if you want to take a side in the coming confrontations, and if so, to decide which side to support. If you choose to stand on the side of democracy, then fear and anger are the two greatest enemies you will face.

Reject Anger. Fight Fear. [RAFF]

Recognize your emotions. When you feel anger, take note of it and identify the cause. If you are being provoked, who is doing it any why? Become clinical.

Any time you feel yourself getting angry, look for the source. Is someone doing or saying something specifically to make you angry. Are you being manipulated? Be thoughtful in your response. In Chapter 8 of this manual you will learn about two tools you can use to help master your threat response: WAIT and WAIST. Study them and learn how to use them to keep a clear mind and move forward.

RAFF. Reject anger. Fight Fear.

It Is Not Your Fault

"Passion can distort judgment, but a commander must wield it carefully—fury directed at the wrong target will lead to ruin." – Carl von Clausewitz, *On War*

The failure to carry the day in November 2024 is not an individual soldier's fault. Figuring out what went wrong—what is going wrong—is not an individual soldier's job. Yes, many of you feel civic and moral responsibility. That's because you are a good person.

Listen up! You voted. You put up yard signs. Talked to friends about the election and urged them to vote. Made financial contributions. You did your duty. Now, it's time to be calm and regroup.

Anger is a trap.

"If your opponent is temperamental, seek to irritate him. Pretend to be weak, that he may grow arrogant." – Sun Tzu, *The Art of War*

"Never interrupt your enemy when he is making a mistake."
– Napoleon Bonaparte

It's time for a reality check. Unless you are a billionaire prepared to throw money into 365-day-a-year political activity, there is very little any individual can do to influence the federal government until the next election. This manual contains several recommendations for building and maintaining morale, including election-related and unrelated activities. But first things first: refuse to be angry.

Your Anger Monetizes Disinformation

The electoral process has been engulfed by a broad range of people and organizations that benefit from angry discourse and clicks in response to fear-mongering headlines. Even if all a soldier is doing is "venting" about some action or the hypocrisy involved in some decision, that outrage is putting money in their pockets.

Understand this, soldier: **Engagement** is the word these merchandisers use to measure their success. They aren't measuring achievement or failure, right or wrong, or the impact of the disinformation they are spreading. All they care about is keeping people online, tuned in, or otherwise "engaged."

They have found, with years of experience and detailed analytics, that the most "engaging" content is the most *angry* content. Therefore, their systems are designed to "promote" angry content. More angry content provokes more anger. It gets promoted. This vicious circle of anger (and the misinformation it contains) is what the sponsor companies call engagement.

NOTE: In discussions about the type of profit-seeking businesses that produce unverified news-like content and promote fear and anger in order to increase engagement this manual refers to them as "angertainment" businesses and part of the "angertainment industry." People who promote angertainment content are referenced as "angertainers."

Advice to the soldier: Study how angertainment works. Observe. Do not engage.

Maintain Your Balance

"We repeat again: strength of character does not consist solely in having powerful feelings, but in maintaining one's balance in spite of them. Even with the violence of emotion, judgment and principle must still function like a ship's compass, which records the slightest variations however rough the sea." – Carl Von Clausewitz, *On War*

It is not difficult to imagine a worrisome, real-life situation that would test the ability to manage emotions. It could be as simple as going on a car trip and having the vehicle break down in the middle of nowhere.

What does a rational person do? Get out of the car and shout at it? Threaten it? Challenge it to "do something" to prove it's worth keeping?

That would be absurd and counterproductive.

What a person will more likely do in that kind of situation is:

- Figure out where they are

- Determine what resources are available: tools, spare tire, communication device with network connection

- Assess the overall situation and devise a plan: walk, call an automotive repair service and wait, try to hitch a ride, walk in the direction where assistance can be found

When dealing with difficult situations, on a real battlefield or in life, there is no room for anger. It will only cloud your vision and impair your judgment.

Evade Capture: Pay Attention to What and Who You Pay Attention To

Attention is, in many respects, a soldier's most valuable asset. Protect it. Use it carefully. Do not let fear-mongering adversaries steal it.

What are you thinking about? What causes worry? How much precious time and attention is being devoted to news and messaging that, as far as the war to defend democracy is concerned, is irrelevant?

The Outrage Machine and The Fog of War

For us to succeed in our defense of democracy, we need to clear away the fog of war and put outrage under control. What is happening on the battlefield must be observed with clear eyes, and we must respond with intelligence. Soldiers must not allow themselves to be driven by fear.

The reality on the political battlefield in America today is that the angertainment industry is producing a thick, toxic cloud of highly engaging, angry content. It is a communication-blocking smokescreen that creates outrage, ambiguity, and confusion on the ground.

As a result, we have difficulty assessing our own capabilities and those of our opponents. We are forced to operate with incomplete information. We are faced with an ongoing, continuously updated, flow of disparagement, ridicule, anger, misinformation, and outright propaganda. Any soldier, caught alone on a battlefield in the fog or war, can reasonably expect to be frightened.

This *Manual* does not suggest that fear should not be felt. We repeat: Anyone who is not afraid of what is happening in Washington today is either not paying attention or is a supporter of the Republican effort to create a one-party authoritarian government in the United States. It is that serious.

There is much to fear. But the response must not be outrage. Anger clouds our vision. It feeds the opposition's angry narrative. It puts money in the pockets of people who profit from angry political partisanship.

Chapter 2
TAKE CARE OF YOURSELF

Withdraw in Good Order

B e kind to yourself.

When the fighting ends, one army claims the field of battle. What happens to the other side, the defeated army?

One of the biggest challenges the commander of a defeated force faces lies in keeping the army together. Remember, the most significant victory for the Continental Army in the American Revolution came in the winter of 1777-78. General Washington kept the Colonial Army together.

The Quartermaster General, Thomas Mifflin, seems to have been somewhat inept, and he was overwhelmed by the challenges of clothing and feeding the troops. The Continental Army suffered from extreme cold, starvation, disease, and inadequate supplies, with thousands of soldiers dying or barely surviving in freezing, ragged conditions that tested their endurance and resolve.

Somehow, General Washington and his lieutenants managed to keep the army together.

In the battle to defend democracy, soldiers won't face those kinds of conditions. When joining up, no one is required to sign an Oath of Enlistment.

In this army, soldiers are allowed to take a break. Go home. Tend the livestock. Chop wood. Take care of family. No one is absent without leave (AWOL). Everyone is a volunteer. Soldiers can come or go as they please.

Retire from the battlefield in good order. Then, soldier, decisions need to be made.

Rest, Recuperation, and Resupply [R&R&R]

The people defending democracy in America today are part of a volunteer army. It has paid professionals in leadership roles, but the troops on the ground are volunteers. Everyone has a major decision to make: Are they going to reenlist?

Take some time. Think about it. Make sure to give yourself a break.

Rest & Recuperation (R&R) – Military shorthand for taking time off to recover from the physical and mental strain of service. It gives people the opportunity to recharge, relax, and maintain morale. Military leaders know that R&R is essential.

Why Do Soldiers Need R&R?

Mental & Physical Recovery – Combat and deployment are exhausting; R&R helps prevent burnout.

Improved Performance – Well-rested soldiers make better decisions and operate more effectively.

Family & Social Reconnection – Time off allows soldiers to reconnect with loved ones, strengthening personal relationships.

Retention & Morale – Offering breaks helps maintain motivation and commitment to service.

Here's our message for you: ***Take a break.***

Now is the time to step back from the fight, recharge, and prepare for the next battle. Resting isn't retreating—it's an opportunity to strengthen yourself for the road ahead.

Disconnect for a While

Avoid news feeds and social media for a "while." You get to decide how long a "while" is.

You will discover two things.

First, you will still be aware of anything truly significant that takes place; and you will be pretty much in touch with everything else, as well. Information is everywhere; you can't totally escape it. But you can reduce the amount of time you invest in monitoring it and as a result, spend less time worrying about the state of the world.

Second, you will find out that you are happier. You'll have more time to enjoy all the "other" things that are going on in your life. Carrying the weight of the world around with you is a big job. Leave the task to others for a while. You'll be surprised how much lighter you feel.

Finally, when you do choose to re-engage you can be more selective about how much news you ingest and you will likely have a better perspective on the world.

Reconnecting with Friends

After deployment, soldiers often seek to reconnect with old comrades. They use veteran networks, reunions, and social media to find former members of their unit.

The same approach is needed in this army. Think about the people who have been worked with on political causes. Is it possible to have more to talk about than the aftermath of one election or preparations for the next? Those personal connections are exponentially more important and valuable than online connections.

Are there people soldiers have worked with that they liked but never got to know? Maybe now, during a lull in the battle, time can be found to reach out and connect with them.

Reporting Back for Duty

When a military unit returns from deployment, it undergoes "reconstitution," which involves:

Rebuilding strength – Replacing personnel and equipment lost in combat.

Training & retraining – Ensuring soldiers are prepared for future missions.

Reintegration – Assisting troops in adjusting back to structured military life.

As warriors for democracy, the details may differ, but the same principles apply. Reestablish connections, reconnect, and build up the unit's strength. Voter registration, anyone?

Training and retraining? There are suggestions in the following chapters about new tools and weapons to use in future campaigns. Unless a soldier is an employee getting paid for the work, there is leeway here. If the CO (commanding officer) hasn't sounded Assembly, leave can be extended.

Of course, you may feel you want to get back into the fight right away. But this was a major defeat. It was truly disheartening, and the aftermath has been unimaginable. A significant portion of campaign rhetoric centered on the devastating consequences of losing the 2024 election. And then it turned out to be much worse.

Take your time. Take care of yourself. Here is something to be absolutely sure of: No one will miss their opportunity to get back into the fray if that's their inclination. The war will still be raging.

Chapter 3
REESTABLISH THE CHAIN OF COMMAND

Choose Your Branch of Service

Professional soldiers are trained to stick together. Even a small unit has a better chance of survival than a lone soldier cut off from the main force. The people working to defend democracy in America today don't have that kind of training.

Armies also thrive when they have great leaders. A charismatic leader like Alexander of Macedonia (a.k.a. Alexander the Great) can use political skill in combination with military expertise to amass an overwhelming force. Napoleon used a similar approach. Other great generals—Hannibal in the Alps or Leonidas leading his Spartans—used their military genius to overcome great odds.

The people working to defend democracy in America today are in disarray. There are a number of possible leaders available, but the defenders of democracy have not yet coalesced around a standard bearer.

Leadership matters.

Going into an election, the leaders are known—the names at the top of the ticket. After the election, the person at the top of the ticket becomes the de facto five-star commanding general on one side. Aides are selected. Campaign promises are recited. The war goes on.

Meanwhile, what happens to the losing army that has been left in disarray?

Identify Your Chain of Command

Are you in charge? Are you the person trying to pull the forces together, reestablish order, and plan for the next campaign?

Probably not. More likely, you are one of the grunts, dogfaces, or wounded warriors, trying to find your way through the fog of war and trying to make sense of what just happened.

So, what should be done?

First, take care of yourself. Rest. Recover. Don't be stupid.

Then figure out where you are. Locate your comrades in arms. And very important: Find your leaders.

It is in the nature of democracy, this ongoing search for leaders. Even when there is someone to respect who is in command, other people are also being evaluated for their leadership potential.

Since you are dealing with professionals—people who run for election to earn their living—you will soon be flooded with information about this or that person. And since this is a volunteer army, there is opportunity to listen to what they have to say.

It's strange, but in a way, it's almost like the days of yore. In Europe, a well-armed knight might check out the various kings and princelings in the area and pick out one with whom to align. Choosing who to follow in those days was a very big decision.

It seems that it is just as big a decision in these modern times of electoral jousting.

Where to Look for Leaders

Start at the top of the ticket. Is there still alignment with the losing general? Is their banner still worth following? In the dark days after a major defeat, the answer may be no.

Check out other elected leaders. Are there people to admire who seem to know where they are going? Do they have a plan? Look around, and maybe someone will be found. The distance is still too far from the next big stages in the electoral process—the primaries—but it's impossible not to imagine how this or that person might fit in the role of commander in chief.

Where will you find them?

They are professional politicians. They will find you.

Grandstanding

Some politicians will say or do things to get your attention. If it makes you angry, it's angertainment. If it makes you think; if they have a serious message, then pay attention to them.

Recently New Jersey Senator Cory Booker set the record for the longest speech in the history of the U.S. Senate. It was a political stunt; a good political stunt. For one thing, Booker pushed segregationist Strom Thurmond out of first place in the verbosity (length of a solo filibuster) standings. Additionally, Booker was talking about real issues and concerns—not reading pages from the phone book.

Booker represents New Jersey where he has pulled other "stunts" in the past. The most famous one: While he was mayor of Newark, he made his residence in a notoriously dangerous housing development in the city. He was putting himself in the same place that a lot of the city's poorest people occupied.

We have not studied Booker's career or positions deeply, but our reaction to his latest stunt was positive. He has worked hard as a public servant. He's done some impressive things, he's making some waves and getting some publicity and he's doing it in a way that we respect.

What do you see when you peer out from your foxhole? Is there a leader you want to follow?

We all need to keep our eyes and ears open. Look for people who can lead. Look for people who reflect your values. When you are ready to re-enlist, offer your sword to the leader and get ready to go back into the fray.

NOTE: An important thing to remember. Any time you become aware of a Democratic politician; the angertainment industry will become aware also. While you may be forming your first impression based on reality, angertainers will be filling airwaves and the Internet with angry, fear-inducing content designed to tear them down.

Pundits and Commentators

There is an astonishing amount of very good writing and other forms of commentary available today. Substack, especially, seems to have a large number of thoughtful people covering and discussing the political scene.

Would it be a good strategy to find some people who seem to align with democratic values and sign up with them for the duration?

As long as there is no nominee or elected official to put faith in, the idea of joining up with an independent leader may be best. In reality, that strategy has worked well for Republicans. Rush Limbaugh, for example, was the drum major for the party for more than two decades. Today, people like Joe Rogan have become political "influencers."

Does it make sense for Democrats to identify and listen to and support some of these smart, dedicated Democratic analysts?

That could be a very good idea, with one caveat: When finding a leader and signing up, take advantage of it by cutting down on input from other sources. Turn off and tune out the rest of the noise. Be aware, yes, but do not listen to or look at everything. Pay attention to what you pay attention to.

Remember: Your time is limited. Conserve your resources. Pay attention to what you pay attention to.

Decide Where and How to Join Up

It is part of the democratic process: This ongoing search for leaders. When you are ready to reenlist, the odds are good that you will already be peppered with fundraising solicitations. You may take a passive role as a financial contributor. The election industry will appreciate that.

Better yet, see if there is a local political organization or campaign that you can join where you meet people in real life. Open yourself to the possibility of gaining new friends and comrades though your shared concern.

Chapter 4
CONDUCT A THOROUGH AFTER ACTION REPORT (AAR)

Learn from Your Mistakes

Mistakes happen. It's inevitable. There are times when, over time or with more reflection, things can be seen differently. **There is one big thing to remember: You are allowed to change your mind.**

In the world of American politics today, it may never be possible to disassociate from Position A. There are people who will accuse soldiers of flip-flopping when they support Position B. Individual politicians can pay a serious price for doing it—changing their minds. Maybe that's the way it is for politicians. But individual soldiers can change their minds.

When *The New York Times* makes a mistake, the newspaper will frequently print a correction. Anything like a misspelled name or misquoted title can earn a few lines in the paper.

Political movements should do the same thing.

There are times when politics gets in the way of common sense. There are times when extremely poor decisions are made that come to be regretted. And on the macro level, the Democratic Party has made some very costly blunders.

Admit Your Mistakes

Here are positions associated with Democrats that have become huge liabilities. We were wrong about some things and we need to own up to our mistakes.

1. Free Speech on Campus

Democrats say they encourage and tolerate and encourage free speech. Democrats support the First Amendment to the Constitution and say that we need to be able to talk about problems freely in order to solve them.

Colleges and universities are supposed to be hallowed sanctuaries for academic freedom and associated free speech. And yet, in the past, controversial conservative speakers have been disinvited from speaking engagements due to student protests. Speakers who actually make it onto a campus event may face protests and be shouted down.

Conservatives, seeking to be disruptive, are frequently involved in organizing speaking engagements for speakers they know are going to spark protests. It's great publicity for them.

University administrators deserve the first round of blame and shame. They are supposed to be supporting academic freedom. They are allowing censorship instead. Blame them.

The college and university faculty deserve a round of shame and blame. There are more of them than administrators. They are closer to the students. They should be fighting for free speech just as hard as the old-timers were back at Berkeley in 1970. Remember—it was the "Free Speech Movement."

And the students? What the heck? They are taking one of their most valuable possessions—their attention—and wasting it protesting against allowing someone to talk. Academic freedom includes free speech, people.

Some people say they are "free speech absolutists." The meaning isn't entirely clear. Scenarios can be imagined where responsible academics could say that a certain speaker was not welcome. At the same time, those imaginary scenarios would be very, very rare. For the most part, playground logic applies: Sticks and stones may break bones, but free speech will never hurt me.

No one has to listen. No one has to attend. There is a right to protest just as the speaker has a right to speak. One does not negate the other. So yes, it's complicated. But to try to ban speakers because of what they say and believe is a flagrant violation of the Golden Rule.

Democrats and academics earn an F on this part of the civil liberties report card. On their behalf, we apologize.

2. The DEI Movement

The intentions behind all the activities that fall under the diversity, equity, and inclusion umbrella were, are, and will be good. One good result is that businesses have profited.

Research has shown that DEI initiatives have improved company performance and profitability. Companies with diverse executive teams are more likely to outperform their competition in profitability. Employees who feel included are more engaged and have less turnover. Overall, DEI initiatives help businesses attract top talent, improve decision-making, and enhance brand perception.

There was a problem with all this: The label (DEI) and the fact that there are these initiatives. When there are initiatives, people are chosen to go forth and spread the word. When there are initiatives, targets are also set up for people who are looking for ways to subvert all the good intentions.

A lot of education has been done. Once people have learned something, it's very hard to make them "unlearn" it.

In Defense of DEI: The War on Empathy

In the meantime, we need to confront the people who see empathy as weakness. Empathy is, according to one of the current angertainment administration's experts, the fundamental weakness of Western civilization. Others argue that excessive compassion leads to societal self-destruction, especially when it comes to immigration.

What are the weaknesses in this kind of thinking? First, the anti-empathy advocates have, at least initially, targeted people we don't know or at least are unlikely to know. The anti-empathy proponents do as much as they can to dehumanize the people they target. The targets aren't your relatives, friends, or neighbors, they reason, so why should you care? Anti-empathy experts cast broad claims of suspicion over the people they want to criminalize and deport. They label Americans we might feel empathy for as criminals, weak, lazy, or otherwise unworthy of our concern.

The DEI initiatives of the last decade were very simply an effort to apply The Golden Rule to workplace culture; to give everyone a chance. In some cases, it was done well. In too many other cases, DEI initiatives were led too zealously or implemented awkwardly.

It was this implementation problem that has allowed the anti-empathy forces to attempt to rewriting the Golden Rule in the workplace. For them, it reads: Do unto others as you would have others do unto you unless the others are unimportant, in which case do anything you want to them.

3. The Pronoun Issue

Pronouns are an excellent example of weirding (see Glossary.) People who are used to using the old fashioned him and her, his and hers words feel uncomfortable when someone says they want to be called "they." It is strange, to them, seems odd.

For people who are unfamiliar with the concerns about pronouns; the shifting use of pronouns can just seem a little weird. It might make them uncomfortable.

There are two possible sources for anger and confrontation due to pronouns.

First, if someone identifies their preferred pronouns and another person ignores their preferences, it can lead to unnecessary conflict and anger. Well, soldier, remember your first responsibility: do not get angry. Perhaps the person is weirded out. Perhaps the person is careless or silly. Perhaps the person is a jerk. Does it matter?

Pronouns are words. They will not hurt you. If you run into conflict over the words that are used around you, your mission requires you to gather intelligence (maybe this person really is a jerk!) and remain calm. RAFF. Resist anger, fight fear.)

Second; give a thought to your own responsibility. If you are choosing to use pronouns that are unfamiliar to other people; then you are the person creating the potential disconnect.

Third: Please understand, it is not easy to keep up with pronouns, even when people try. Here's a list of pronouns that people are using today. Some are easily recognizable. Others are unfamiliar to many people. In alphabetical order: ae, aer, aers, any, all, co, cos, eir, em, en, ens, ey, fae, faer, faers, he, her, hers, him, his, hu, hum, hus, it, its, ne, nem, nirs, per, pers, she, sie, sier, siers, te, tem, ter, thee, they, thon, thons, thou, ve, ver, vers, xe, xem, xyr, yo, yos, ze, zir, and zirs.

Dealing with Pronouns

If someone indicates that they want to be identified in a particular way—from the spelling of their name to the pronouns they want used to refer to themselves, then kind, polite people (typical Democrats) will try to accommodate their requests.

In some instances, people will fail to respond appropriately. There are lots of possible reasons why the response might be "wrong" to the person affected. The pronoun user may just mess up, or may make a mistake, or may be told by an editor to use a different word. The pronoun user may also be a rude person who is using words to express their anger or some other negative feeling. They might be jerks or worse.

If someone is trying, give them a break. They are nice people and they are trying. If they are jerks—well, now you have more information about them. That is valuable intelligence, soldier. Now move on.

Under these or any other circumstance, they are words. They will not hurt you unless you choose to let them hurt you and make you angry. Is that a power over you that you that you want to give them?

4. The Transgender/Sports Issue

This could be the single biggest mistake Democrats have ever made.

Inclusion and inclusiveness are part of the Democratic DNA. When children want to participate in sports, they should all be included, and so, of course, transgender girls (people who were born male and who have undergone hormone replacement therapy) should be allowed to participate in girls' sports. That is the position that countless people and groups representing Democrats and Democratic Party interests have taken.

Here's the problem:

Sports is all about competition—**fair competition**. In wrestling, for example, a 110-pound wrestler isn't going to compete with a 187-pounder. Wrestling has weight classes to ensure the competition is fair. High school sports teams generally compete in divisions of some sort where schools with enrollments of a couple hundred don't compete against schools with enrollments over 1,000. The big idea always is to make competitions fair.

There is plenty of evidence to show that men have a physical advantage over women in a wide range of sports. Consider the elite performers in sports such as swimming and track; in directly comparable events, men perform significantly better than women.

In recent years, there have been some great examples of girls who have competed against boys and been very successful. There was a girl in Maine who won a state wrestling championship competing against boys. It's rare, but it happens. And when it is a girl stepping up to compete against young men, it is certainly a fair competition.

But, when the equation is turned around and someone says that a person born with a male physique, skeleton, and musculature can go on a drug regimen and then compete against girls—some people want to say that's okay? It is not. It is, in fact, a form of "doping."

Hormone replacement therapy (HRT) is used to reduce a trans girl's testosterone level and introduce estrogen to create a female "hormone profile." It is scientific, but it's not a science. There is no way to know how little or how much this treatment will affect any individual.

In practice, HRT does reduce the athletic performance of trans girls. So it works. But how much does a trans girl's performance have to be reduced to create fair competition with other girls?

That is an impossible question. Anyone who says they have an answer is spinning up a rationalization to support a position they hold.

Unfortunately, with all the issues in sports around the world related to doping, it is unreasonable to introduce HRT, a form or controlled doping, to allow a special group of athletes to compete in what is essentially a "lower weight class"—the girls' teams. It is unfair.

Everyone deserves the opportunity to compete in sports. Perhaps there will be a day when there are enough trans girls to have their own competitions. For now, they ought to be able to "move up" and compete with the boys. That will always be fair. But trans athletes need to recognize that when chemical treatments are involved, there may be limits placed on their "rights" to compete in some sports.

Democrats need to acknowledge that doping, whether it is to done enhance or to reduce and athlete's performance, is unacceptable in competitive sports.

Period.

5. Democratic Leadership and the Biden Health Situation

This was all about fear. The party was misled in many ways about President Biden's condition and ability to campaign effectively. Then a magnificent opportunity to see democracy in action was wasted.

Original Sin by Jake Tapper and Alex Thompson, the book that documents Joe Biden's health and age-related issues, makes it painfully clear that President Biden was not fit to serve four more years. Some people might have even have made a reasonable case for removing him from office. Clearly, he should have been encouraged to stand aside sooner to make way for a new candidate via the Democratic primary process.

That didn't happen.

When, when he finally was finally persuaded to step aside, a second huge mistake was made.

Democratic leaders were afraid. The election was coming soon. They needed to have a candidate right away because they were afraid there wouldn't be enough time for a modern, billion-dollar roll-out and advertising and branding campaign. There wouldn't be enough time to saturate America with frightening images and angry fears of what would happen if the wrong person was elected.

Here's the saddest part about this failure. Democrats had a perfect opportunity to show democracy in action. They had a convention scheduled and ready to go.

Their problem: Democratic party leaders were afraid to let a candidate be selected by the Democratic convention. And so, they resorted to old school, behind the scenes politicking and Kamala Harris was anointed as the candidate. We all know how well that went.

Here is what could have happened. Potential candidates could have been identified and vetted in the weeks leading up to the convention. Then, in one of the most-watched events in event in television history, Democrats could have nominated candidates. Viewers could have met a half dozen or more very good candidates.

Convention delegates would have voted in a meaningful selection process. They likely would have had to vote and gain, and maybe again.

Suddenly, the convention that has devolved into a meaningless television advertorial would become an actual news event.

It would have been fantastic. It would have engaged huge audiences. It would have introduced a wide number of serious Democrats to a national audience. It would have diverted attention away from the angertainment-centered Republican campaign. It would have set the stage for a truly great, democratic election.

Unfortunately, Democratic leaders were afraid.

Reality Check

Soldier—do you think the 2024 election was bad? Imagine how much worse it would have been if the opposition was running a candidate who was not a convicted felon and all the other divisive baggage associated with the current president. Landslide doesn't begin to express the size and scope of the victory that a less divisive candidate might have claimed.

Believe it or not, it could have been worse.

Chapter 5
KNOW YOUR ENEMY

It's More Complicated than You May Think

Study this chapter carefully. You may believe you know who your enemies are. You may think they are Republicans.

You are wrong.

Rank and file Republicans today are human shields.

Your real enemies – our opponents in our work to save democracy, are base human instincts and emotions that are being used by individuals and businesses to enrich themselves, evade responsibility for their actions, and subvert democracy.

The Axis of Evil

We have already identified fear and anger, the basic "engagement" forces harnessed by Angertainment, Inc., as our greatest enemies.

There are, however, two additional forces that sit at the heart of the opposition to democracy: greed and hubris.

Greed

Greed is central to the American economic system. Big business in America has developed an extraordinary ability to earn profit. At the same time, the executives who operate those same businesses have learned how to reduce the "expense" of paying people for the work they do. The extraordinary profits earned by American companies go in an ever-increasing proportion to the wealthiest people in America and the world.

At the same time, companies replace workers with machines, reduce benefits paid to workers, resist efforts by workers to form unions, and resist efforts to provide workers with a government-backed social safety net.

At the same time, greed drives corporate actions and policies that have environmental, health-related, and social costs that the companies avoid paying. Examples of this range from the opioid crisis, to the financial meltdown to 2008, to global warming. Whenever concerned citizens identify the negative consequences of corporate action or inaction, the companies resist and refuse to accept any responsibility. Why? Greed. If they accepted responsibility for their actions, it would cost them some money.

The American economic system is rigged. It's designed to help rich people get richer and to put poor people at a disadvantage. Employment for middle class workers is increasingly being changed from "career" opportunities into "gigs." And even if someone has a "gig," they may also need a "side hustle" to get by financially.

Curiously, the greed factor also leads to an increase in "white collar" lawlessness in areas including self-dealing and de facto bribery of government officials, various forms of financial fraud, insider trading, and government-enabled tax evasion.

A thorough analysis of the role of greed in America today is far beyond the scope of this small *Manual*. Common sense, however, tells us that people with great wealth have inordinate power in America, that they are reshaping our government to help them amass even greater wealth, and very little of that wealth "trickles down" to ordinary citizens.

When you assess a situation, soldier, ask yourself: "Who is getting paid? Where is the money going? Who benefits?" Follow the money and assess. Fair compensation or greed?

Hubris

The 2024 election unleased a tidal wave of hubris that has swept over Washington, DC. People with no expertise or experience in government have been given extraordinary power and responsibility. Decisions are made based on a few people's "gut instincts." Science or research are unnecessary; the people who are in charge just "know" things, and they are reshaping policies and programs to suit their beliefs.

One of the key elements of hubris is the way it eliminates any sense of shame. People with great hubris can do something, see it fail, ignore the failure or lie about it, and move on without having any sense of failure or shame. They view themselves as omnipotent.

Hubris leads to faulty decision-making. Hubris leads people to surround themselves with sycophants. Hubris causes leaders to attempt to suppress criticism. Hubris leads to corruption and cronyism. Hubris leads to the erosion of democratic norms.

As we move forward, we want leaders who are intelligent enough to understand and act on intelligence. We don't want people who lead with their guts; we want people who use their brains.

How the Axis of Evil Works

The Axis of Evil is a vortex—a swirling, synergy of greed, hubris, anger, fear and lies that creates chaos and confusion while giving the people who are orchestrating it a place to hide.

Fear and anger provide emotional content. Greed provides motivation. Hubris allows people to willfully ignore their truth and bend government to fit their personal needs or whims, and benefit from it.

Angertainment, Inc., resides at the center of the axis of evil. It operates like a turbo jet engine, sucking in information (some of it true, some not) and fueling it with fearful warnings, dire predictions, ridicule, sarcasm, misinformation, and sometimes, lies. Then they polish it and make it look as realistic as possible.

The highly engaging "output" from the angertainment industry is fed into social media channels that are designed to amplify its reach and emotional impact. Social media is the afterburner that multiplies the negative impact of angertainment content.

And—this is important—this stream of "content" is everywhere. It operates all the time. It is inescapable.

The angertainment industry monetizes fear and anger. It supports hubristic elected and appointed leaders. These intimately connected forces generate huge amounts of money, rewarding the individuals involved in the processes; encouraging their greed.

American Democracy's Other Enemies

The Republican Party

The Republican Party is now under control of the angertainment industry. Conservative Republicans candidates for office are famously subject to attacks from even more conservative Republicans in safely gerrymandered districts.

If Republicans step out of line – compromises on something or agrees with a Democrat on an issue – it could be the trigger that sics the angertainment industry on the them. If a high-ranking angertainment favorite in government says a Republican is being disloyal, the impact can derail a Republican politician's career.

Therefore, Republican "leaders" generally remain silent. They run and hide from taking real responsibility. They have been effectively neutered by the system that has given them so much power.

Republicans have some of the same enemies as Democrats in this regard. But the risks to Republicans are much greater because the angertainment industry has so much influence in Republican primary elections.

Republicans are also imbued with a kind of hubris that allows them to cheat and game the system where democracy is concerned. This is most obvious in the efforts to disenfranchise Democrats through gerrymandering. Yes, Democrats will work to create favorable districts. Republicans, however, have raised gerrymandering to a fine art and are willing to fight as fiercely as possible to reduce or even eliminate Democratic representation in statehouses and Congress. And they are proud of it.

Republicans have also taken action to reduce the power of Democrats when they lose elections. Legislatures in North Carolina and Wisconsin, for example, took steps to reduce the power of Democratic governs in their states when Republican candidates lost gubernatorial elections.

Republicans are capable of a kind of naked partisanship that puts Democrats to shame.

Democrats play by the rules. Republicans, when they can seize an advantage for themselves, change the rules.

Features of the Modern Republican Party

Here are two additional characteristics of Republicans you need to be aware of and understand.

The Grover Grovel – A great majority of Republicans including more than 80 percent of the members of Congress sign on to Grover Norquist's Taxpayer Protection Pledge. In doing so, they promise to oppose any increase in marginal income tax rates for individuals and businesses. Additionally, they agree to oppose any net reduction or elimination of deductions and credits unless matched dollar-for-dollar by further reducing tax rates.

It is a kind of "we want a free lunch" pledge. No matter what is going on or how great the need is, we don't want to pay for it. Massive tax cuts that have chiefly benefitted wealthy people are sacred. It is a position that it contributes to gridlock and undermines fiscal flexibility, especially during economic crises.

Hypocritic Oath – Republicans, working closely with the angertainment allies, have mastered the art of hypocrisy. They will say one thing one day and another the next. They will contradict themselves and laugh about the inconstancy. The bottom line: they will take whatever course of action they want to take or are told to take regardless of any past commitments. Hypocrisy is a feature, not a bug.

The lesson for you, soldier, it his. Do not get angry or feel outrage when a Republican does something hypocritical. They have taken a solemn oath to do exactly what they are doing.

The Election Industry

Elections have become a huge business in America. There are experts, pollsters and advertising mavens who all have to be paid. And the messages they produce, specifically negative campaign advertising, falls into the realm of angertainment.

To understand this, you just have to follow the money. Consider the following presidential elections.

1960~$20 million
Kennedy vs. Nixon; spending was modest and mostly party-driven

1980~$92 million
Reagan vs. Carter; public financing capped spending

2000~$528 million
Bush vs. Gore; rise of soft money and PACs

2020~$6.37 billion
Biden vs. Trump; record-breaking spending by candidates and outside groups

The overall cost of elections in 2020, adding the money spent on state and local elections, was about $14 billion. The election industry was paid about $90 per vote for everyone who participated in the election.

There is a word for this: Insane.

If we compare an election campaign to a wartime air raid, our spending on elections would be enough to bomb every square inch of the electorate a dozen times over. Our elections produce a massive deluge of messaging, most of it fear-inducing and angry—that simply adds more fuel to the angertainment industry's furnaces.

The overall cost of the 2024 election was a little more than $15 billion. Any reasonable person would look at it and say: It is insane.

Friendly Fire

Friendly fire is a serious concern for Democrats—friendly fire coming from the election industry.

It is tough being targeted by political opponents and the angertainment industry. Why do we have to receive fear-mongering, angry messages from people who we generally think of as our friends? People we generally support? The reason is simple: it's what the fund-raising industry knows how to do. They have experience doing this. It works.

The basic approach is to scare the daylights out of donors so they pony up more money.

We recommend putting a fear/anger filter in place for fundraisers. When you receive a fundraising message that is too much like angertainment, unsubscribe. Opt out from the mailing list. And be sure to leave a comment to tell the candidates and fundraisers why you did it.

Demand to be treated like an intelligent human being. Send them this kind of message: "Educate and inform us. Encourage us. Don't try to scare us. We are already scared."

Ourselves

"We Have Met the Enemy and He Is Us"

Walt Kelly's famous quote from the comic strip *Pogo* originated on a 1970 Earth Day poster to highlight environmental issues. It applies equally to political challenges.

Sometimes the enemy is internal: Democratic infighting, purity tests, and circular firing squads. Friendly fire—Democrats attacking other Democrats—can either be angry and fear-inducing, or it can be informative.

When talking amongst themselves, soldiers are going to gripe. They are going to complain. They will have their reasons, and we should treat them seriously. As you go through the rest of this manual, you will find your Marching Orders. Study them carefully. And follow them—even when you are dealing with fellow Democrats.

If we are going to drive fear and anger out of our politics, we need to start with what's happening in our own house.

Chapter 6
KNOW AND SUPPORT YOUR ALLIES

Friendships and Alliances are Important

If it were not for France, the American Revolution would probably have failed. We can be certain the colonial army would never have won the decisive Battle of Yorktown without the aid of French troops, ships, artillery, and supplies.

Real allies should be like real friends—people you can count on when the going gets tough. It is vitally important to recognize and support your allies.

Real Journalism

Truth matters. Support real journalism—the kind that involves verification of facts, consideration of multiple sources, editorial oversight, and accountability. Subscribe to legitimate news organizations. Pay for quality reporting.

Real journalists follow verification protocols before publishing. They issue corrections when they make mistakes. They distinguish between news reporting and opinion. They provide context and multiple perspectives.

Learn to distinguish real journalism from propaganda and angertainment. Real journalism makes people uncomfortable on all sides because it reports facts regardless of whether those facts are convenient for any particular narrative.

The implosion of the newspaper has been hard on the journalism profession, but many of reporters, dedicated to their profession, have found new media homes and ways to communicate effectively.

Real journalism is an industry that is separate and distinct from angertainment. Real journalism separates news from opinion and labels them appropriately. It employs reporters who check facts and verify quotes. It's a business that is dedicated to telling you the truth.

If you still have a local newspaper, subscribe to it as well as to the best online news services. Extend your support to non-profit journalism including public radio and television programming. They are important allies in charge of communications.

Unions

Organized labor has been one of the most consistent defenders of working people and democratic values. Unions fight for fair wages, safe working conditions, and worker rights. They provide a counterbalance to corporate power.

In 1950, salaries and benefits for working Americans were better, on average, than today. Workers got raises every year. Many companies offered pensions. If a CEO announced layoffs, there was shame attached. People could reasonably expect a long, stable career. In the 1950s and early '60s, about 30 percent of American workers were members of unions.

Union jobs set the stand for what a "good" job looked like. It would include fair wages, good benefits, medical insurance, regular salary increases above the rate of inflation, and a pension.

That sounds like a dream today. One of the biggest changes in the American economy has been the decline in union memberships. The Republican Party has waged a long war on unions that has sapped their strength. The resistance to efforts to form a union today has been strengthened so much that even when workers win a union election, companies can brazenly refuse to negotiate a contract.

Times may be changing, however. The fact that workers at places like Amazon and Starbucks are working to establish unions suggests that conditions may ripe for a revival of interest in unions. Look across the Atlantic to countries like Denmark and Finland where 60 percent or more of workers are union members.

Unions and union members can be among your allies. It will be helpful to learn a little union history, too. People bled and died for the right to have a union in the United States. That experience and history is an important part of the DNA of the Democratic army.

Smart, Thoughtful People

Much of the recent government activity has been aimed at "dumbing down" decision-making. Why should you talk to experts, conduct research, or listen top advice from anyone when we have "gut instinct" to lead us. All that research and consideration will just slow us down.

In reality, the efforts to bypass research and careful consideration are primarily driven by greed. Follow the money and see who benefits. Those "gut instinct" decisions are very likely going to financially rewarding for the decision makers and their friends.

Part of our job, in supporting our allies, is to encourage smart people to keep going; to identify good ideas and help people find them in the middle of the "fog of war" created by the angertainment industry.

Authors, Thinkers, and Academic Institutions

Support writers, researchers, and educational institutions that produce thoughtful analysis and preserve institutional knowledge. Subscribe to their newsletters. Be a supporter. When you get good info, share it with people who will care.

Scientists and Environmentalists

Global warming is real. It is an existential threat to people, especially poor people, living in certain areas of the world. It is an existential threat to the natural world. Coral reefs, for example, are being devastated by ocean warming the way glaciers are being melted by the air. The climate crisis is exacerbating other environmental issues like habitat reduction and chemicals in the air and all that other environmental concerns. Your support for groups like *The Climate Reality Project* and *The Sierra Club* make a difference.

Yes, we need the organizations that are trying promote sustainability and push back against pollution.

Give them a hand.

Women

With Republicans waging a war on empathy, women may be the most natural allies for Democrats.

Men, overall, have a pretty bad track record for civil behavior. Men commit the vast majority of violent crimes worldwide, including homicide, assault, and robbery. In the U.S., men account for over 90% of homicide arrests and 80–85% of all violent crime arrests. Men make up over 90% of the global prison population. They also have higher rates of reoffending after release.

Men are more likely to binge drink and develop alcohol use disorders. They also have higher rates of alcohol-related hospitalizations and deaths. Men have higher rates of illicit drug use, especially stimulants and opioids. They Men are more likely to gamble excessively and develop gambling problems.

Men are more likely to engage in reckless driving, physical fights, and dangerous sports. This includes higher rates of traffic fatalities and accidental deaths.

Men are, by and large, a mess. Why should they be running the country?

Women are natural allies for people seeking to create and kinder, safer, better world. Learn what they have to say. Support their interests.

Non-White Americans

Has the Jim Crow era in the south really ended, or was it just paused for a while? Some people would like to have us believe that the color of a person's skin doesn't matter anymore. Any serious study of health and financial disparities that includes breakdowns by race will show otherwise.

This nation has a long and sordid history that includes the enslavement of African peoples and the destruction of Native American societies. It's important to remember the past, to understand how things that may have occurred in previous generations can still "trickle down" to impact current generations.

This America isn't a melting pot. It's a quilt, comprised of millions of individual pieces with every one deserving of our care and respect. Build alliances with people from all races. It will make you stronger.

LGBTQ Communities and Groups

Gender issues with things like pronouns and passport identification and caring for trans youth have obscured the most important fact about allies in the LGBT community. They are probably the best organized, most effective civil rights activists in America today.

This can be challenging for people do not have any friends or relative who they know are gay or trans. When people find themselves dealing with something unfamiliar—possibly something they have been told is "wrong"—they may react badly. This is where and understanding or weird and weirding is important. An inappropriate response from someone may not signal that they are racist, sexist, or otherwise prejudiced. It may simply be they are weirded out a little bit. They need to more experience with the idea. Meet with people where they are. Talk to them. Listen to what they say. They could become exceptionally valuable allies.

Aid Organizations

From national aid organizations to your local food back; you will find people committed to working together to make things better for other people. They are all potential allies. Talk to them. Find out what they need. Support them and build coalitions.

Local Political Organizations

Get involved at the local level. This is where change often begins and where individual effort can have the most impact. Volunteer and you are likely to find a group of like-minded allies.

Friends and (Politically Compatible) Relatives

Don't underestimate the power of personal relationships. The strongest political networks are built on genuine human connections, not just shared outrage on social media.

Talk about the axis of evil – anger, greed, and hubris. Talk about angertainment and the fog of war. When you have an existing relationship you have a great opportunity to have a great ally.

Chapter 7
INTELLIGENCE, INTELLIGENCE, INTELLIGENCE

Act With Intelligence

You have a brain. Use it. Don't be stupid.

Do not let anger cloud your vision.

Think before you do and say things related to politics. Shut up. Listen. Respond with empathy and intelligence. Do not shout.

It gets back to the basics: Be who you are.

Our challenge is to avoid getting sidetracked into useless disputes or distracted by people who are shouting at us. The people who are working to undermine democracy are doing things designed to confound us, appall us, and make us angry. Don't let them succeed.

Use your intelligence to assess the situation, and do what you can without wasting any of your precious attention.

Move forward thoughtfully. Be smart and caring—that's who you are.

Gather Intelligence

Intel is critical, soldier. Be alert. Pay attention. Whenever you are talking to an adversary, shut up and listen.

Go further. Pay attention to what is actually happening, not just what is being said about what is happening. Read primary sources. Look at data. Follow the money (who is getting paid? Who is earning profits from the action?).

When you engage in conversations with adversaries, look for HUMINT – military jargon for human intelligence. That's where the focus is on debriefings, interrogations, and "source operations."

The last item, source operations, is an area where significant information can be gathered and it may provide opportunities for identifying targets of opportunity—especially disaffected veterans of the war on empathy. When you talk to people, ask them how they feel. You may also be able to identify coded messaging. Identifying hidden (and not so hidden) meaning and subtext is mission critical.

Use DRT on Your Opponents

DRT (Dread Replacement Tactics) is a high-risk, high reward approach that any soldier can employ. While it is officially considered as part of the Special Operations Command, DRT training is available to all personnel. The operational principle of DRT: Replace DREAD with curiosity.

It sounds simple, but it's not.

Dread is a word that we all understand. In this context, it is appropriate and used with its default meaning. We can also, however, think of it as an acronym.

DREAD equals: Default Reaction: Enraged, Anxious, and Defensive.

DREAD works and spreads the way poison gasses were used by Axis forces in World War I. Conducting operations while enveloped in DREAD is impossible. Soldiers need to learn to defend themselves against DREAD.

DREAD Protection

Any soldier who wants to go on a DRT mission is required to have an advanced ability to minimize fear and exception anger control management. You do not want to call attention to yourself, soldier. Your mission is HUMINT. Remember that. If you react in outrage to the kind provocation spread via the angertainment media, your success on a DRT mission is unlikely.

Here's what you need to do instead. **Replace DREAD with curiosity.**

An effective DRT operation involves three phases: Infiltration; observation & engagement; and debriefing.

First, find your way through enemy lines and get close to people who may be members of the opposition or who may simply be casual observers. Listen to what people are saying. WAIT. When you have an opportunity, ask good questions. Gather information. Then withdraw from the field of battle and think about what you have learned.

What are people saying? Is it true? Are there ways you can engage constructively? Are there insights you can share with trusted friends?

Most important—avoid emotional weight of DREAD. Angertainers and opposition politicians want you to feel bad—that's their game. Don't play it. Instead, be the smart, curious person you are. If you can identify someone who is a likely kindred spirit, maintain your connection with them.

Share Your Intelligence

When discovering useful information, share it with others who can benefit from it. Build networks for sharing verified information. Your communication channels may be electronic. If you're fortunate, you'll also have people you can share with in real life. But don't let it be a gripe session or a replay of the anger and outrage created by angertainers and politicians. Instead, talk about what you have learned by engaging with the opposition.

Use Intelligence Intelligently

Having information isn't enough. It must be analyzed, contextualized, and applied strategically.

The Fog of War

"War is the realm of uncertainty; three-fourths of those things upon which action in war is based are lying in a fog of uncertainty." – Carl von Clausewitz

We are struggling through a time of chaos and unpredictability. It is extraordinarily difficult to move forward with incomplete information and constantly shifting circumstances. Communication channels are jammed with competing messages, competing pleas for funding, and competing claims from people who need attention.

As a result, concentration is shattered by uncertainty, noise, and confusion in communications.

Your challenge, soldier, is to remain calm, assess the situation using all the information you have at hand, offer constructive thoughts when you think they may make a difference, and above all, be true to yourself.

Chapter 8
ARMAMENT

Active Defenses for Democracy

The current assault on Democracy has developed into a war on three primary fronts. The people opposing our constitutional are deploying fear and misinformation. They are proceeding with great hubris and are satisfying their greed by enriching themselves.

They have launched a war on empathy. Our opponents say Americans need to be hard-edged and care less about other people; especially people who live anywhere except in the United States. Additionally, we should not care so much about poor people. Or disadvantaged people. And if there are people in the United States who cannot prove that they are properly "documented," then they are enemies too, and must be hunted down and deported. Empathy—the application of the Golden Rule—is weakness, they say. They believe that murder, as long as it means killing people they think should be killed, is justified because they say it is justified. And with that, they paint the

United States of America as a nation that condones and perpetrates murders.

They have launched a war on truth. Our opponents' misrepresentations and, frequently, outright lies, have overwhelmed the abilities of fact checkers. The angertainment industry has amplified and repeated falsehoods so effectively that a significant majority of Republican team supporters believe them—all of them.

They have launched a war on justice. The judicial system is being used to pursue political vendettas against companies, universities, and individuals. At the same time, a broad array of convicted politicians, fraudsters, rich people, and the tourists who attacked police forces and broke into the Capitol building, have all been pardoned.

Our challenge, as defenders of democracy, is to protect ourselves by standing behind our principles and beliefs where we can be who we are. The idealism that has pervaded the American Dream for so long will absorb most of their anger.

Additionally, when facing their attacks, we have tools we can use to defend ourselves and our democratic ideals. The following section of the manual describes the attack vectors that we face and the tools we can use in our defense. Additionally, the *Manual* will provide several useful defensive measure that can be used on an ad hoc basis in various combat situations

The War on Empathy

Republican-aligned voices are increasingly saying empathy is a liability rather than a virtue, especially in political and cultural debates.

They say empathy is a "the fundamental weakness of Western civilization." Religious leaders say empathy is acceptable only when deserved and warn against "indiscriminate empathy" that undermines moral clarity. Influencers describe empathy-driven politics as emotionally manipulative and harmful to national interests and as "cognitive vulnerability."

The general approach that our opponents are taking is to try to oversimplify complex problems in areas like immigration, criminal justice, and social welfare and resolve them with simplistic, frequently cruel, and in some instances, inhumane solutions.

Golden Rule, et. al

The Golden Rule is a moral principle, an ethical guideline, a philosophical proposition, and a religious teaching. It describes two sides of one coin, referring to a concept that exists in nearly every religion.

For Christians, it is a positive statement. In Matthew 7:12, Jesus says, "Do to others what you would have them do to you."

The Jewish iteration comes to the moral dictum from an opposite perspective. Rabbi Hillel the Elder said: "That which is hateful to you, do not do to your fellow." This phrasing is useful. It reminds us that there are times when defining this wisdom as a prohibition makes more sense.

Asian religions have their versions of the Golden Rule too. Confucius taught, "Do not impose on others what you do not wish for yourself." The Hindu *Itihasa says* "This is the sum of duty: do not do to others what would cause pain if done to you." The Buddhist Dhammapada says "All tremble at punishment. Life is dear to all. Put yourself in the place of others and harm none." The Taoist Golden Rule: "Regard your neighbor's gain as your gain, and your neighbor's loss as your own." From Nigeria, a Yoruba Proverb says: "The way we treat others is the way others will treat us."

These expressions show that the Golden Rule isn't just a Western ethical idea — it more like global moral intuition, adapted to different cosmologies and social structures. It is powerful, and it is a dangerous problem for people working to undermine democracy.

They justify cruelty by saying they are being rational. They urge us to apply the Golden Rule selectively – only with people who *deserve* empathy. And they say that empathy has been *weaponized* by Democrats and others—that Americans today have too much empathy.

The Empathy Challenge: When you are engaged with someone in a discussion on a question that involves a kinder outcome versus a cruel one, summon up your preferred iteration of the Golden Rule. If the Golden Rule does not apply, then why? Where do your opponents find the exceptions that allow them to employ cruelty instead of treating others the way they, themselves, would want to be treated if circumstances were reversed.

The War on Truth

Truth matters. Always. Even when it's uncomfortable. Even when it's not convenient. Especially then. The truth, supported by verifiable facts, is the foundation of all effective action.

The Republican war on truth has been raging for decades. Republicans and their angertainment industry allies have a simple approach to dealing with uncomfortable truth: They deny it. Simple, easily visible reality can be distorted and history can be rewritten simply by repeating a falsehood over and over again.

For the angertainment industry, verisimilitude is very important. Angertainment is in the business of creating content that looks like news. We describe it as "truth-like." It is not, however, necessarily true. Angertainers rely on a mixture of truth and true-sounding content. They manipulate it to make it as engaging (anger- or fear-provoking) as possible. They then distribute it as widely as possible to get as much engagement (money) as possible.

What the angertainment industry does not do is verify that its content is true. Angertainment companies don't have reporters on the ground developing sources, checking facts, and taking the steps necessary to be sure stories are accurate. Instead, they are ready to take unverified content ranging from press releases to impressionist versions of actual news to entirely speculative conspiracy theories, and present them as though they were true.

There is no way to "win" an argument with someone who truly believes in their alternate view of reality. There is, however, a way to casually challenge them and perhaps, over time, persuade them that there is such a thing as truth, and that they can find it being provided by real journalist—not angertainers.

The Reagan Rule: Trust but Verify

When someone repeats a possibly outrageous, possibly false claim, ask: "Where did that come from?" Then follow up with: "Do you think they verified that?"

From there, quote Saint Ronald Reagan: "You know what President Reagan said: Trust, but verify. That is what real journalists do."

The Reagan Rule is a tool that you can use to reduce the damage caused by the distortions and conspiracies spread through angertainment and social media sources. It's a teaching tool. Talk about the beloved Republican and how to use his advice.

The War on Justice

The Republican war on justice is being waged on multiple fronts. In one area of action, you find the entirely extra-judicial murders of alleged drug smugglers in the Caribbean and Pacific. No war has been declared, no court has tried or convicted anyone, and the Americans responsible for ordering these murders have not provided any evidence about the people they are targeting. The entire sum of the judicial procedures being used is as follows. These are bad people. We won't tell you how we know that, but they deserve to die so it's okay for us to kill them.

The war on justice is also being carried out in the United States where the Justice Department is carrying out judicial attacks on people who the current president of the United States does not like. America's respect for justice is also being undermined by the egregious use of the presidential pardons for people who were justly and fairly convicted of crimes.

All of this is against the background in which the United States is the world's leader in incarnation, and in which there is ample statistical evidence that the existing judicial system is weighted against poor people and minorities, while it is soft on white collar crimes and tax evasion.

Justice and Empathy

The American justice system is flawed, but it has, over time, tended to get at least slightly better. Then the current angertainment administration took control in Washington. Today, with old inequities joined with current misuse and abuse of judicial proceedings, the American promise of "justice for all" is ringing hollow.

The Sixth Commandment Plus the Golden Rule

The murders of boat crews in international waters, far from the coastline of the United States, can be challenged with one of the messages that Republicans believe should be present in public spaces including schools.

The Sixth Commandment addresses it. In the King James Version of the bible, it says "thou shalt not kill." Modern scholars working on the translation of the original biblical Hebrew prefer to say: "thou shalt not murder" which leaves open the option for killing in war or as a judicial proceeding.

In either interpretation, the biblical admonition would apply to these extrajudicial killings. And so, once again, we can ask about where Christian apologists for the current administration can find the asterisk or exception written into this important Christian commandment. Apparently, as our opponents see it, the commandment ought to be rewritten: Thou shalt not murder, unless (insert rationalization here).

Additional Defense Measures

Following are a number of defense measures you can take in any situation where you have an opportunity to engage closely with an opponent. There depend in large part on our nonviolent overall strategy of engaging constructively with opponents who still retain the ability to0 listen to and understand common sense.

WAIT: Why Am I Talking?

WAIT is an acronym like RADAR, SONAR, and LASER.

WAIT stands for: **Why Am I Talking?**

Listen. Ask questions. Don't interrupt. Conduct field research. Listen to what people, including opponents, are saying. Don't make it a debate. Don't try to persuade anyone. Just listen carefully and respond with empathy. Spend a little time walking in the other person's shoes.

WAIST

WAIST is, LIKE WAIT, an action-guiding acronym that is especially important in combatting angertainment and misinformation online.

It stands for: Why Am I Sharing This.

When you receive a particularly engaging message on social media or e-mail, you may find yourself saying "hell, yes" and immediately sharing it.

Danger!

If you want to be part of the solution and NOT part of the problem, you should WAIST it. Ask yourself: Why am I sharing this?

To assist you in working this, measure your impulse against an international standard created by Rotary International, a global network of over 1.4 million members in more than 200 countries, dedicated to humanitarian service, ethical leadership, and advancing peace through thousands of local clubs and international projects.

The organization adopted the Four-Way Test as guide to dealing with any matter, including challenging moral and ethical problems. To pass the Four-Way Test, someone must answer all the questions affirmatively.

The Four-Way Test

Is it the truth?

Is it fair to all concerned?

Will it build goodwill and better friendships?

Will it be beneficial to all concerned?

Before you share anything, ask yourself those questions. Can you verify that it is true? Is it fair—especially to any other people involved. What impact will it have—will it build goodwill? Or will it incite fear or anger? Will it spread misinformation? If you were talking directly to a friend, would it help make your friendship better.

In summary, will sharing this "content" be beneficial to everyone touched by the message. Is it really something you need to comment on or share. After you apply the four-way test, you might realize that it is not.

Angertainment, especially, is created to be highly engaging. Angertainers want you to share everything they say—that's how they earn their money.

Do you really want to help them?

Follow The Money

Any time anyone does or says something that seems difficult to understand, break it down and try to figure out who is benefitting financially. There may be political influence in play, but most of the time, there is someone or a group of people who have a financial interest in "whatever." Once you know who's benefitting financially, many other aspects of a situation may be much more clear.

Thou Shalt Not Shout

Effective soldiers always remain calm in the face of battle. In this war of ideas and nerves, remember do not get angry and shout. No one ever had a sincere change of heart because someone shouted at them. Do not shout. DO NOT SHOUT ONLINE. Do not shout!!!!!!!

Don't Talk About It: Show It

When talking about complicated things, obtain charts and graphs and other visual aids to explain things. Words are just words out there in the air. Provide a picture. Everyone has sat through PowerPoint presentations—they use visuals. The same should be done in political discourse.

Arm yourself with a deck! Create visual representations of the issues that matter. Show data. Make the complex understandable.

Respond with Humor

Humor and satire are friends, and they are healthier than anger. When talking with teammates on the sidelines, feel free to mock the other side. Repeat the late-night jokes. Laugh at the absurd hypocrisy. Laughing releases pent-up energy without the negative effects of anger.

Humor can be employed when talking to the opposition too. Think about using self-deprecating humor: "I don't belong to any organized political party. I'm a Democrat." Avoid sharp jabs. Keep it light.

Have Some Fun

Meet up with friends in real life as much as you can. Don't be angry—push back against the fear mongers. Sing songs. Talk about what the late night comedians are saying.

The angertainment industry is producing a blinding fog—a poisonous cloud of anger, resentment, personal insults, and ridicule aimed at all of us. And it is profiting handsomely. Don't put money in their pockets.

Find your friends—your buddies and like-minded souls. They are out there. Build connections. Share your worries (just not all of them). Keep it light. Have some fun.

Chapter 9
STRATEGIC PLAN

Reduce Hostility. Engage Thoughtfully.

Strategy: Win elections by building a stronger, more resilient democratic coalition.

Tactics: Empathy; Trust, But Verify; Sixth Commandment; WAIT; WAIST; and above all, Be Who You Are

Objective: Reduce the level of hostility, resist attempts to undermine fair elections, and rebuild democratic norms.

Siege Warfare

Look at our position. We are defenders. We have to build and maintain a strong defense against the people who are undermining our we can benefit by studying the strategy and tactics of 19th Century siege warfare.

The people inside a castle or walled city had several goals.

First—They had to survive. They had to defend themselves from curses, arrows, rocks, and by the 1800s, bullets and cannon fire.

Second—Protect their most important/precious people and possessions. The people outside the walls were likely going to loot and burn the city if they prevailed.

Third—Confuse and resist the attackers. Deny them intelligence about your supply situation. Use straw men or fake cannons to make them think your defense is stronger.

Fourth—When possible, conduct sorties. Lead teams of people blow up defenses or lay mines. Put snipers in the field. Make every effort to disrupt the enemy.

Fifth—Wait the opposition out. Be strong. Stay calm. Keep morale inside the walls as high as possible. Never give up.

Sportsification: The Team Mentality Problem

Here's the challenge: Elections have devolved into a bizarre kind of sporting event. People who vote no longer consider the merits of a Democrat versus a Republican. They simply look out at the playing field, see who is wearing the uniform for the team they root for, and vote for that person.

Sports and sports fans provide a useful analogy. Imagine being an Ohio State football fan with a friend who is a

Michigan fan. Now imagine the scenario in which thoughtful consideration and logic are used to convince the friend to switch allegiance from Michigan to Ohio State.

What would it take? The answer is easy: *It can't be done.*

"Fan loyalty" is baked so deeply into many people's psyches. Changing it is impossible. You might pay your friend a million dollars to switch side and root for the Buckeyes. The friend might take the money and show all sorts of outward signs of becoming an Ohio State booster. But deep inside, the friend is humming *"Hail to the Victors"* (the Michigan fight song) while cashing the check.

Yes, there might be a few undecided voters, but they are becoming increasingly rare. Attempts to "convert" voters to switch from one team to another are very unlikely to succeed. That kind of effort is probably making individuals less likely to support the other side in any way.

The Election Industry is making every effort to be sure this is the case. The consultants, pollsters, and fundraisers are all trying to "lock in" their constituents. And the angertainment industry is helping in the "lock down" effort by creating the highly profitable, unverified news-like content that both blinds and entertains its audiences.

What Can Be Done

If converting people is impossible, what smaller, more achievable things can be accomplished?

First: Find good leaders and support them. The election Industry, despite its flaws, employs lots of experts who have a lot of experience running election campaigns. We need to support them with campaign contributions and, when possible, field work. When you find really good leaders, you sometimes create a scenario where you opponents wish they were players on their team. They might even vote for them.

Second: Find your kindred spirits. Look for people who are aligned with your values and think about ways you can work together. It might be something as simple as just becoming (or remaining) good friends and doing friendly things; talking on the phone, having lunch, going to a game. Gather a few more like-minded souls and think about what you can do to make a difference; having a lunch, dining out, going to a game. Talk about some of the ideas in this *Manual*. Talk about angertainment. Share the Reagan Rule. Discuss ways to keep empathy alive as a value and virtue—not a weakness.

Third: Be who you are and engage intelligently. Don't argue over anything. Just listen and be curious. Ask questions like: "Are you sure of that?." Remind people of the Regan Rule: Trust but verify."

ASAP: All States Are Purple

Angertainers and the election industry like to talk about "Red" states and "Blue" states. There's a long history behind that color coding. Today, it seems like it's permanent.

It's not. It's not permanent. And it's not even correct.

Here's the truth: All states are purple.

The whole red/blue business is a product of politicians, pollsters, and the television industry from back in the pre-Internet days when television was the at the top of the media food chain.

Gerrymandering is a major factor in the red/blue divide. Republicans, in particular, have implemented computer-designed political districts to minimize the probability that Democrats can win elections. The gerrymandering may "pack" as many Democrats in one district they are willing to concede, so the votes won't impact neighboring districts. Or they may "crack" areas that have large numbers of Democrats so the votes are diluted, spread into other districts, so that Democratic voters have little influence.

But improbable is not the same as impossible.

And even when you may not be able to win in a local or regional district; you can still work to tip the balance in statewide elections.

Infiltration and Guerilla Warfare

Be who you are. Replace dread with curiosity (DRT). Ask questions and listen. (WAIT). When you get good, useful information, share it. (WAIST). So gather intelligence intelligently, and be aware of possible chinks in the typical Republican's armor. Are they a little too empathetic to be a good Republican today?

Use the word angertainment. Talk about Angertainment, Inc. and what you think about it. Identify islands of common ground. You might be surprised how many of them there are. And you can share your feelings—tell someone what it is like to live in a country where you, as a Democrat, are reviled, accused of any number of crimes, and where the top Republican has advertised that he would like to shower you with feces. Tell them how that makes you feel.

Undermine precarious arguments. Don't engage in debates; just ask about sources of information and how people verify them. Be yourself. Be curious. Do not get angry.

Decimate the Republicans

People who for the so-called Republican "base" are, we expect, unreachable. But there may be some people less engrossed in angertainment who might be moved by logic and reason. There are probably a few Republicans who don't think that empathy is a weakness. There are likely a few Republicans who will acknowledge that some things, shouted by Republicans at Democrats are not true. It is possible that you might find a weak link in the lockstep march of Republicans to the angertainment industry's beat.

The Republican positions today on many issues are mean-spirited and cruel. Additionally, they want to minimize or eliminate programs to support low-income individuals and families. And they say things about race and gender that upset nearly anyone who is not white and straight. The truth is that Republican positions on a wide range of topics are unpopular.

Is it possible that one in ten Republican-leaning voters might be persuaded that they would be better off voting for a Democrat?

It is possible. And that is the proper definition of decimation; going for one in ten. You are never going to persuade the die-hard angertainment addict to vote in favor of democracy. But there are other Republican voters who can be reached. Maybe as many as one in ten. Maybe more.

Election Work

The fundamental work of democracy continues: voter registration, phone banking, canvassing, poll working. This work matters and will matter more in future cycles.

Get in touch with your local political organizations. You can work for the party or find an election campaign for a good person. Invest your time and earn the satisfaction of being a difference maker.

Peaceful Protest

The right to peaceful assembly and protest is fundamental. Use it wisely and effectively.

Join in on a few protests. Be calm. Meet like-minded strangers. Listen to speakers if the sound system is good enough. Show up. Be counted. And along the way, have some fun.

Spend Time IRL (In Real Life)

Spend more time meeting, working, and talking to people in real life—not just online. Start simple. Learn people's names and use them. The clerk at a store. The person behind the fish counter. The new neighbor. Be who you are. Be friendly. And think about wearing a big button that says you are a proud Democrat.

You Can't Un-Ring a Bell

One effect of the effort to increase diversity, equity, and inclusion in the workplace has been measurable business results. The evidence is clear: organizations that move closer to the kinds of goals that DEI programs encourage do better. They make more money. Employees like working in those places better.

The general idea behind these initiatives was to educate people, to increase everyone's awareness of challenges, issues, historic trends, and more.

Unfortunately for people who think these efforts are evil, people can't be "un-educated." Back in the 1960s, when working for civil rights, people talked about consciousness-raising. It was one of the goals of the movement. And it worked. Once a person knows the history, nobody can cause them to un-know it.

The current political assault won't eliminate efforts to increase diversity in work environments; it will simply drive it underground. DEI will evolve, over time, into something that will simply be known as good business practice.

The same principle applies to other areas: civil rights, climate change, economic justice. The education has happened. The consciousness has been raised. That can't be undone.

Chapter 10
RULES OF ENGAGEMENT

Be Who You Are

We cannot emphasize this enough. You are an intelligent, caring individual. You support Democracy as it has evolved over more than two centuries in this county. You are aware of its many imperfections, including its history of inequality and prejudice; it's not perfect, but we can all agree it has been getting better. Unfortunately, today, some of the ground we gained in the quest to form that "more perfect union" has been lost.

Our challenge is to work effectively to end the threats that the current angertainment administration poses and put the nation back on the path toward becoming a country we call all—every American—be proud to call our home.

The most important power in all of this belongs to you. Be who you are. Assemble with like-minded people. Get to work.

What Democrats Believe

We care about people, starting with ourselves and those close to us. But we also care about people we don't know, including those in the United States and around the world. As American citizens, there has always been a belief that when dealing with Americans, you were working with the good guys in any story. American history has taught that this hasn't always been the case. But we can try. As Democrats, we want our country to be a leader, standing on the side of justice and compassion and supporting the interests of ordinary people everywhere.

We care about the world—Planet Earth or *Spaceship Earth* as Buckminster Fuller labeled it. Plan A is to follow the science, listen to people who actually know what they are talking about, and work to save the world from overheating. There is no Planet B. We must work together to preserve the planet.

As Democrats, we know we are an imperfect nation—a work in progress. The aim is to always keep trying to be better.

Hope for the Best. Prepare for the Worst.

The war to protect American democracy continues. Spring is coming. The defenders of democracy will reassemble. Stronger. Smarter. Tougher.

Keep Going

The most powerful weapon available is attention. Use it wisely.

Be a good soldier. Be a good follower. Be a democracy supporter.

It's Complicated

Busy people want simple solutions, and they are willing to vote for people who mouth platitudes and promise they'll fix things with a snap of their fingers. Reality is more complex. Democracy is messy. Good governance requires nuance, compromise, and patience.

Accept the complexity. Work within it. Don't promise simple solutions to complex problems. We need to keep reminding people of this.

Cooperate

"I don't know. What do you think?"

"Let's see if we can work on this problem together."

These phrases are powerful. They invite collaboration rather than confrontation. They acknowledge uncertainty while maintaining commitment to finding solutions together.

Marching Orders

Go forward with clear eyes and full hearts. Stand on the side of democracy.

Remember Valley Forge. Remember that the Continental Army's greatest victory was simply staying together through the winter. Do the same now.

Rest when you need it. Return when you're ready. The defenders of democracy will reassemble. The work continues. The mission endures.

E pluribus unum.

1. Fear Less.

Your fears for American democracy are real and justified. The challenge for you now is to understand that new reality, address the assault on democracy when possible, and at the same time, maintain a clear head and move forward. The enemies of democracy want to goad you, make you fearful and angry. Do not let them succeed.

Pay attention to what you pay attention to. Don't allow your precious attention to be captured by fear-mongering politicians and their parasites in the angertainment industry. Do not allow your mind to be clouded by fear, anger, or hate. Undertake dread replacement tactics—displace dread with curiosity.

Do not feed the trolls. Do not amplify your fear via social media. Dop not monetize angertainment content by clicking on it, commenting or sharing.

In other words, be yourself. Be the person with a clear understanding of what fear is and its negative consequences such as anger and paralysis.

Prepare yourself to push your fears aside and work for democracy.

2. Be Kind.

The occupying forces in Washington are waging a war on empathy. They want people in the United States to believe that The Golden Rule, an ageless test for empathy, is conditional. They want Americans to believe that some people deserve empathy and others do not; especially if they are poor, non-white, or anyone else they deem "undesirable."

They think The Golden Rule should have an asterisk. It should only apply to a few people. The Golden Rule, as they understand it, does not apply to strangers or anyone who pushes back against their efforts to undermine democracy.

We believe that empathy is an essential element in our humanity. Do not allow yourself to be conditioned to cruelty and callous disregard of human life.

Be yourself. Live by the Golden Rule.

3. Play Fair.

The occupying forces in Washington are waging a war on justice. People who have been convicted of crimes ranging for facilitating money laundering and drug dealing to assaulting police officers and breaking into the U.S. Capitol Building have been pardoned. The Department of Justice has been transformed into tool for political retribution. Justice in America has become a commodity that can be purchased by wealthy or influential people or doled out to political allies. The legal system, from police forces through to the court system and into the post-conviction realm of clemency, has been corrupted.

There are people among the opponents of democracy who want to have a Christian moral code in the form of The Ten Commandments posted in schools and public places. And at the same time, people in Washington D.C. want to make us see the Sixth Commandment—Thou Shalt not Murder—as "optional." They want to legitimize extrajudicial killings. They want to legitimize murder as a political tool.

We need to ask ourselves who we are.

Do you believe in justice and fairness? Are you a murderer?

Be who you are. Support justice. And if the opponents try to change the rules in the middle of the game, calmly, deliberately, push back as hard as you can.

4. Tell the Truth.

The occupying forces in Washington have declared a war on truth. White house officials routinely say, tweet, and share false and misleading statements. They rarely, if ever, issue corrections or make retractions. Additionally they create confusion by making policy statements without the enactment of any policy, and they unilaterally defy policy decisions that have been enacted. They have replaced truth with uncertainty.

Truth matters. We may want to believe what people tell us, but is it true? Follow the dictum popularized by Ronald Reagan: Trust, but verify.

Truth can be complicated at times. There is context and nuance to be considered. Whether listening to voices from your own side to the battle or to voices from elsewhere, insist on understanding what is true.

Be who you are. Trust what people tell you, but if there is any doubt, verify it.

5. Say You're Sorry.

We all make mistakes. We think things, say things or do things that we regret. Everyone makes mistakes. It is important to know that. It is important to identify mistakes when you make them, so you don't keep repeating them. It's also important to admit your mistakes. And to help move forward in the right direction, it never hurts to say you're sorry. In the realm of politics, it seems that nobody ever wants to admit they are wrong about anything. It opens them up to political attack.

In our world, as the troops on the ground, we can afford to admit we are human. Saying you're sorry isn't a weakness. It's a sign that you are a thoughtful human being who can learn and grow from a mistake.

Be who you are. If you make a mistake that impacts someone negatively, say you're sorry.

6. Share Wisely.

In life in general, and especially in the online world, think about what you are sharing when it strays into news and politics. Remember WAIST: Why Am I Sharing This, and the Four-Way Test. Remember that your clicks, shares, likes, and the time you spend "engaged" online are earning big companies more money. Social media platforms will do everything in their power to capture one of your most valuable assets—your attention.

Be who you are. Think for yourself. And be careful what you share. Don't feed the trolls.

7. Form Up Ranks.

Leadership matters. Pay attention to leaders who seem to share our concern for democracy and your values. Share positive information and good stories. And at the same time, pay attention to your local political situation.

Remember: ASAP. All States Are Purple. Find like-minded people in local political organizations. Work with them. Establish connections in real life. No matter what the conditions are on the ground, there is useful work you can do. Find leaders you believe in and people you trust. Make your engagement in the battle to defend democracy about more than money—financial support for candidates. Use your intelligence. Infiltrate. Conduct guerilla warfare. Own up to it; you're a Democrat. Be yourself.

8. Engage Strategically.

Pay attention to what you pay attention to. Push back against attempts to goad you into clicking and experiencing angry content. If something was bad the first time, don't watch a lot of reruns—more reports about the same thing and the follow up opinion pieces. Be aware of what's going on in general, but you don't need to know all the details.

Use your attention wisely. Share wisely. Donate money wisely. And whenever possible, engage with people in real life. Wear a button that says you're a Democrat. If anyone asks you about it, tell them why.

Learn people's names. When you're having a routine conversation with someone in real life like a sales associate or a cashier, ask them their name. If they have a nametag, thank them by name. Don't hunker down. This isn't trench warfare.

Smile. Talk to people. Be yourself.

9. Have Some Fun.

Despite the best efforts of the occupiers of the White House, we can't live in constant dread. Your marching orders stress the need to resist anger, replace dread with curiosity, and move forward intelligently and strategically. You can even have some fun when you're on duty. Join up with friends for a protest. Go ahead and share stories from the Baby News Network and surviving late night comedy hosts. Use laughter to displace anger.

And when you are not on duty, be yourself and for goodness sake have some fun. Do things you enjoy doing. Do stuff with friends and family. Keep up your own spirits and cheer up the folks around you.

Be yourself and have some fun.

10. Vote.

Okay, that's what this whole democracy thing is about.

We think we live in a pretty good country. It's imperfect, but over time, it's gotten better. We've been heading in the right direction. We got to this point by being a democracy. We had elections that mattered. There were three branches of government that balanced each other in what civics textbooks called the separation of powers.

We ended the enslavement of human beings. We pushed back against racism, we believed in education. We learned a lot about the world through science. We acknowledged problems, and we worked to find solutions that were fair to all concerned.

They—the opponents of democracy in the current administration—say that we live in a terrible country and that they alone can make it better. They believe empathy is bad because, for example, it gets in the way of deportations. They believe that murder—including the premeditated killing of two men who remained alive in the wreckage of an alleged drug boat—is justified.

They believe that it is acceptable for elected officials and people close to them, to mix business deals with foreign policy. They believe that it is perfectly okay for the president of the United States to trade pardons for profits.

The occupants of the current White House believe that they should win the next election and every election that follows it, and they are attempting to change voting maps and voting laws to help make that possible.

And they believe that they have the right to send militarized forces (ICE, National Guard, and the regular armed forces) into American cities and states in order to assert their control of the population.

The bottom line, American democracy in imperiled.

We Democrats believe in democracy. We are facing an extremely serious threat.

Are we going to be the United States that helped win World War II and that served as a beacon for democracy in the 20th Century? Or are we going to become an authoritarian state with a government that aligns itself with dictators, ignores war crimes, enriches elected officials and their allies, and mocks the idea of American democracy?

Be who you are, soldier. Fear less. Be kind. Tell the truth. Play fair. Say you're sorry when you make a mistake. Share wisely. Form up ranks. Engage strategically. Have some fun along the way. And when the precious opportunity comes around, vote.

ADDENDUM

Addendum: Request for Armament

During the Revolutionary War in the American colonies, basic equipment was in short supply. General Washington's troops lacked such basics as food and shoes.

In today's political environment, people who support democracy have other essential needs. We respectfully submit the following requisition to leaders of the Department for Defense of Democracy. We believe these resources would add significantly to our armament. Additionally, they would help our troops avoid distraction and focus on their mission.

Scoreboard

We need to be able to keep track of the enemy and the destruction it has caused. Presently, there are resources dedicated to tracking some aspects of the current administration's damage.

We would be well-served with a central location where links to all of these individual sets of records and information are being maintained.

We need to be able to clear our minds to remain positive and hopeful. Tracking the damage in our heads makes this difficult. Give us a central location—a website somewhere—where we can identify categories of destruction, measurements of it, links to background information and what efforts are being made to reduce the negative impact.

A Democracy Deck

Ross Perot was right. It's easier to understand complicated problems if you have visual aids: good graphical representations can tell a story more effectively than words.

We want to encourage all our leaders to provide us with the best available graphical representation related to all of our major issues.

We can think of it as a PowerPoint or Keynote Deck.

For a good example, look at the "deck" prepared by Al Gore for the Climate Reality project. Or just look at the astonishingly informative graphics prepared by serious journalists today by the New York Times, Washington Post, and other professional news sources.

Most Americans carry a compact presentation device in their pocket today. We would help our soldiers in their mission, especially when engaged in efforts to address and subvert the impact of angertainment, to equip us with a curated set of materials they can easily locate to display and share via their mobile devices or computers.

www.ingramcontent.com/pod-product-compliance
Lightning Source LLC
Chambersburg PA
CBHW060531080526
44586CB00012B/695